SPEED READING

A Guide To Rapid Learning And Memory Acceleration How To Read Triple Faster And Remember Everything In Less Hours

Descrierea CIP a Bibliotecii Naționale a României
FOSTER, JESSICA

Speed Reading. A Guide To Rapid Learning And Memory Acceleration How To Read Triple Faster And Remember Everything In Less Hours. – Bucharest: My Ebook, 2018
ISBN 978-606-983-599-9

159.9

SPEED READING

A GUIDE TO RAPID LEARNING AND MEMORY ACCELERATION
HOW TO READ TRIPLE FASTER AND REMEMBER EVERYTHING IN LESS HOURS

**My Ebook Publishing House
Bucharest, 2018**

CONTENTS

Chapter 1. KNOW WHAT SPEED READING IS ALL ABOUT 13

Chapter 2. EXERCISES TO IMPROVE SPEED READING ... 19

Chapter 3. FACTS ABOUT SPEED READING 25

Chapter 4. WHAT IS SPEED READING ABOUT? 33

Chapter 5. WHY COMPREHENSION IS DIFFICULT. WHY COMPREHENSION AT A FAST SPEED IS DIFFICULT AND HOW YOU CAN OVERCOME IT.... 36

Chapter 6. IMPORTANT REASONS WHY YOU SHOULD LEARN SPEED READING 45

Conclusion 49

INTRODUCTION

I want to thank you and congratulate you for buying this book; **Speed Reading: A Guide To Rapid Learning And Memory Acceleration; How To Read Triple Faster And Remember Everything In Less Hours.** This book has proven stops and strategies on how to **Speed Read and Comprehend Faster.**

This book will make you spend lesser time, more than 80% cut, to study and comprehend faster than you used to.

Thanks again for purchasing this book. I hope you enjoy it.

Copyright 2018 by Zen Mastery - All rights reserved

This document is geared towards providing exact and reliable information in regards to the topic and issue covered. The publication is sold with the idea that the publisher is not required to render accounting, officially permitted, or otherwise, qualified services. If advice is necessary, legal or professional, a practiced individual in the profession should be ordered.

- From a Declaration of Principles which was accepted and approved equally by a Committee of the American Bar Association and a Committee of Publishers and Associations.

In no way is it legal to reproduce, duplicate, or transmit any part of this document in either electronic means or in printed format. Recording of this publication is strictly prohibited and any storage of this document is not allowed unless with written permission from the publisher. All rights reserved.

The information provided herein is stated to be truthful and consistent, in that any liability, in terms of inattention or otherwise, by any usage or abuse of any policies, processes, or directions contained within is the solitary and utter responsibility of the recipient reader. Under no circumstances will any legal responsibility or blame be held against the publisher for any reparation, damages, or monetary loss due to the information herein, either directly or indirectly.

Respective authors own all copyrights not held by the publisher.

The information herein is offered for informational purposes solely, and is universal as so. The presentation of the information is without contract or any type of guarantee assurance.

The trademarks that are used are without any consent, and the publication of the trademark is without permission or backing by the trademark owner. All trademarks and brands within this book are for clarifying purposes only and are the owned by the owners themselves, not affiliated with this document.

Chapter 1
KNOW WHAT SPEED READING IS ALL ABOUT

There are several ways to retain information in our brains. We can go through bulk information, a lot of pages and yet memorize these details without any difficulty. Yes, it is possible; I have had several questions about this before, and I have been a beneficiary of these techniques, they work, they are real.

Speed reading is the series of methods that are used to increase the rate of reading without affecting the rate of retention and understanding. This technique can be very effective as it is a sure guide to encourage anyone who needs to cover large bulk of materials in a short duration.

Speed reading claims that by using any of its techniques, you are sure to double the speed of your reading almost immediately. And with constant and frequent practice, your reading speed can exceed 10000 words per minute.

The principle of speed reading has been for a long time coming; up until 1940, there were training machines that could help anyone interested in his to speed read. The device that had been used to check for the speed reading rate was the tachistoscope. This equipment is sensitive as it can detect and identify images that just appear for a few milli-seconds, that is about 2ms.

There are some components that are used to help learn the technique of speed reading.

1. Choose the right environment.

Environments matter a lot, and it is the corner stone to faster assimilation. It is better and easier to assimilate information in a serene and quiet environment than in a noisy place. Distractions can reduce your retention ability, and this will affect the attention you give to the information you are reading.

A poor environment can be a major disadvantage to speed reading. When there are distractions around, then your attention to the piece you are reading will drop. And this will drastically reduce your speed. A good analogy is the cars we drive around, the speed of the car increases when it stays on the acceleration for a longer time. But if there is a stop in the process, then the car must accelerate again before it can get to the initial speed it already had.

2. Position yourself at the Right Distance.

The distance between your eyes and the material you are reading matters a lot. When your books or laptop screen becomes too close to your eyes, then it will affect the eye adjustment mechanism. This can make the eyes to become lazy quickly.

3. Learn to skim smartly

This is the initial or somewhat superficial vision; it is done by simply searching the paragraphs for any relevant information that may help understand the paragraph. Skimming helps to remove the words that do not add meaning to the information being read.

4. Sub-vocalization is a big no.

This is the first technique that is being taught to anyone who desires speed reading. To be truthful, once you master this art, then you will notice a remarkable increase in your reading speed. It is also the hardest technique to learn. This technique has not only been found to increase learning, but it has also been seen to help the eyes to increase its field of vision.

The main reason why sub-vocalization reduces reading is based on the fact that sub-vocalization is just a silent way of talking to ourselves. and the words we speak are limited to about 300-400 words per minute; hence until we break the habit of sub-vocalization, then we may not be able to increase our reading speed and reach our desired rate.

5. Meta-guiding

This is the use of some object, sometimes the finger, to move along the text as your read along. This helps to increase the field of visual as it increases speed reading. Some methods have proven to be highly effective than others, that is using the pointer along the pages in a linear motion or the moving them zigzag along the pages on the piece.

In every of the process mentioned above, try not to backtrack. This does not only reduce your reading speed, but it affects the assimilation and speed reading. Going back to re-read a line or a paragraph is not advisable.

Speed reading is a useful tool, and it helps to study more efficiently. It can decrease the needed time to memorize details and comprehend any info. Personally, I have observed a remarkable increase in my reading speed; I had doubled my reading speed in the first week of practice. However, the efficiency of your reading speed is largely depended on the nature of the material that you should memorize and retain. As for novels and stories, these two categories are not heavy with technical terms hence speed reading has proven very successful for me.

Chapter 2
EXERCISES TO IMPROVE SPEED READING

There are several exercises that can increase your reading speed, but amongst the many exercises that there are, I will select the most effective four, explain them further and the special cases when they should be used.

These exercises, however, should not replace the routine speed reading practice that you ought to take in order to improve your reading speed. There are also several paid courses to learn speed reading, however, be rest assured that the information in this book will guide you through the appropriate steps to increase your reading speed. You should improve your reading speed by practicing everything in this book at your own pace, and this will not cost you any penny.

Hand Technique

To practice these speed reading exercises correctly, you will need to learn with a very simple text that is easy to read. Use your finger to trace the bottom as you read along. The main reason for this is to keep track of your pace just as you read along with your finger. Just begin with your regular reading pace with your finger and then increase it as you go along. This will give you a drastic effect on your reading speed, and if done faithfully, you can create a remarkable impact on your reading speed in 7days.

Sweep Reading Exercise

This is the main work in speed reading. It helps you read ideas instead of words. In sweep reading, you would see a large bunch of words at a glance and understand what these words talk about. And instead of reading each word or sentences, you grab the information in a short paragraph and make progress as you move along. Also, as the hand technique, you will need to make use of your finger as a pointer. However, in this case, instead of using the finger to swipe across the lines as you read, you will have to read through the middle of the paragraph downwards. This method is the key to speed reading, and it will help you read the words in a large bunch than by words.

Card Technique

The major problem in reading is the habit of back reading and going over the line you have just read maybe to get the meaning of a new word or the whole sentence. This card technique exercise is used to increase the reading speed, and the improve comprehension in the long run. It will also help you remove the wrong habit of going back to check up words or sentences for whatever reason there be. In this exercises, you will need a card or a blank paper. You will use this card to cover every line that you have finished reading; this will prevent you from going back to check any word that you have just passed. As you do this, endeavor to read quickly as you can but try not to be too fast so you can get the meaning of the text.

Zigzag Technique

Use this method after you have properly mastered the card technique. Remember when you were much younger in elementary school, you were taught how to read texts from left to the right and to ensure that you do not miss any word in a sentence. Well, this is exactly the opposite of the zigzag method; here, you will have to read your text in a scattered manner, sometimes from right to left and bottom to top, this is important because it will help you know how to grab the necessary details of the text. Reading the left-to-right patter will delay you and has its own negativity. However, from this zigzag method, you will understand how to look at a paragraph and then you can pick out the information in it, with just a glance.

In all these exercises, remember that daily practice is the key to mastering the act of speed reading. There are no short cuts, howver, if you follow these steps as listed in this text daily, then you should experience a marked improvement in your reading speed in 7 days. This should be up to 1000 words per minute. Yes, it is that effective.

Chapter 3
FACTS ABOUT SPEED READING

There are lots of programs that can show the qualities of being a good speed reading program. These programs sometimes can be beneficial; however, there are several disadvantages of using these kinds of programs to learn speed reading. Just so I stress the point again, be rest assured that everything you need to know to become better proficient in speed reading is already placed in this text. There is no need to enroll in any more onsite programs or online courses if the details of this book are followed strictly.

Also, before you begin this practice, you should have in mind why you need to learn speed reading. Are you a student in law school? Do you have a lot of novels to cover in short period? Or are you running behind schedule in your course work and need to cover a lot in a limited time. Any of these reasons could be a good motivator to stay through the whole speed reading exercise. It is important to first point out the reason for the speed reading before embarking on any of the exercises.

Major Bad Habits that can delay Speed Reading Process

Firstly, there are the eyes skip back; we have spoken about this initially. It has to do with the habit of looking back to words and sentences just to catch the idea of what the sentence is saying. This is not supposed to be, as much as possible, do not practice this as it can slow down the reading process.

Secondly, the eye over use; this has to do with reading each word at a time; when reading, you are supposed to read blocks of words at a time and not just one word at a time. This habit can gradually be broken after several speed-reading practices.

Thirdly, Sub-vocalization; this has been mentioned before; it is important we don't sub-vocalize. This can be a major slowing factor for speed read learners.

The process of speed read can be unique to every individual. However, there is a constant and core principle that is associated by the speed reading process. And once this is followed then progress will be made. Unfortunately, there is hardly anyone who achieves speed reading in just 10 minutes. Hence there is a need to get a strong motivation and invest more time to achieving this feat. Once your brain has been trained on speed reading for 7 days, it will catch the techniques and you will speed read effortlessly henceforth.

There are several reasons why people read slowly; some even give excuses for their slow reading habit and thinking that the excuse is worth the slow-reading habit. Speed reading is beneficial to the brain, it aids concentration and help make fast decision.

Some of the reasons for slow reading include;

1. Physical eye defect
2. Poor/inadequate reading practice
3. Sub-vocalization of words
4. Reading paragraphs/sentences more than once
5. Word for word reading
6. Impulsive fear, sometimes of not understanding the information

Having some eye condition can contribute to a poor reading habit. If you notice that there are some conditions in your eyes that may cause you to be concerned then go check the eye with your doctor. It is however advisable that this is done before beginning any speed reading exercise.

Once you have accustomed yourself to reading, you cannot unlearn the process and even if you haven't read anything for a long time, it wouldn't make you not know how to read. You may just simply take some time to accustom yourself with the whole reading process again. You cannot just jump over a novel and begin to speed read when you haven't read for a long time. The ultimate advice still remains; try to add reading to your schedule daily, to catch up with the whole speed reading process.

Many persons (am tempted to say everyone) try to read the information they see in their head, this is a very poor method of reading and it can reduce the speed of our reading. The moment we can handle the speed reading process, then our brains will be able to handle things and information faster. We can only read word for word because that was the method we were all taught; and unlearning that word-for-word habit is key to increased speed reading habit.

Unlike the popular belief, that one need to read slowly to understand, the actual fact remains that we need to increase our reading speed if we want to increase comprehension. A speed reader will just simply pick out the relevant information and remove the junk words that are used mostly by writers to fill the sentences. A speed reader uses key words to read and this is the major component of a sentence, without keywords, sentences will not make sense.

Important information about speed reading is to begin the speed read exercises with books that are large fonts and will not cause too much strain for the eyes to focus on. As a beginner, you need to understand that there is a need to eliminate every factor that can come as a discouragement to your speed reading exercise. Small font texts can just an obstacle. People can get major difficulty with normal or small text fonts.

Also, it is advisable to begin the speed reading exercise with a sample document that you are familiar with. This especially will help you to focus on the skills of speed reading instead of comprehension process.

Do not bother about your comprehension rate. This can be a major concern to anyone learning the speed reading habit. In fact this is the major concern about any speed reading program; the comprehension level. Many are concerned about comprehension rate and how it can be affected by the speed reading practice.

The one way to overcome this fear is to follow the steps as listed above and practice more often. Do not concern yourself with the comprehension rate; it will improve after a while of speed reading.

This is the reason; the brain is in charge of comprehension. At the initial stage of speed reading, it tends to be as if you are reading faster than your brains but it is just the beginning. The brains are going to 'catch-up' with the rate at which your eyes move and follow the words and as soon as that happens, then comprehension would improve.

Chapter 4
WHAT IS SPEED READING ABOUT?

Speed reading is possible for everyone, no matter their reading rate. This is a key fact to note when choosing to learn speed read. Here are some good details to keep tab off before practicing speed reading.

Speed Reading

Speed reading is an important information processing skills that help to improve the brain and eye muscles. The speed reading quickens the pace at which we read and also improves our retention abilities.

Knowledge is power and knowledge comes from reading. There is an increased need for people to read continually, this is partly because we are bombarded with a lot of information daily.

Speed reading is an extremely powerful tool that will help to manage properly, information and time; it will help you add more knowledge and become more efficient.

Speed reading is very useful for learning. It can also help in cases of pleasure and study. Speed reading makes things go faster and better.

Speed reading is for several categories of persons, but these classes of persons are mostly in need of a speed reading habit.

Persons who enjoy reading novels and newspapers

Academic persons; College students, University students, Language Students

Business persons; who deal with reports and proposals.

Speed reading is non-complicated materials, and it is advisable for kids not to get involved in the speed reading exercise mostly because they are just known for reading. Also, children with reading impairment should not be exposed to speed reading; their underlying ailment should be handled first.

Chapter 5
WHY COMPREHENSION IS DIFFICULT
WHY COMPREHENSION AT A FAST SPEED IS DIFFICULT AND HOW YOU CAN OVERCOME IT

The wider the visual range of the eyes, the more words and lines can be covered. This is the first principle of speed reading. Minimized vocalization and sub-vocalization will make reading faster and more convenient.

If you want to learn how to speed how to speed read and this is not first book you are reading about it, you must have read several bad and negative articles about it and how it is difficult to comprehend while you speed read. Many talk about the impossibilities of getting comprehension at this speed. But this kind of idea is seen in several persons who have neither practice the speed reading or rather were given a wrong training about the exercise. Many have tried to achieve the training and still get super fast comprehension alongside. Hence they are quick to lose hope and give up the practice so quickly.

For effective reading, and getting comprehension means that your whole mind has the power to read, interpret and respond accordingly to the stimuli of the print. Now, comprehension does not mean saying the words aloud and repeating them to yourself, in fact, the fact that you repeat these words is a sign that there is no comprehension. Hence, just as stated before, if the words are vocalized, it will limit the speed limit no matter how fast you are.

We all create habits and in order to get new habits, we have to create and build new effective habits and imprint them on our mind as a direct response to the print that we read. Every speed reading activities will help you to build these habits as well as teach you a perfect eye moving technique that will guide you through. However, only a few contents will give you the ropes on how to successfully do this in order to increase your rates.

However, the problem of comprehension at a high reading rate is usually associated with these factors.

1. The comfort zone of the brain: the brain learns by habit. Hence when the brain learns at a comfortable speed it is likely difficult to leave this comfort zone and forge ahead. Also, more seemingly you are functioning at just a fraction of the brains capacity. Anything can be understood by the brain at 2 to 10 times faster than the current rate you are using now. The more the brain is exercised, the more it

improves. This is the same reason I have emphasized the need to daily practice and routine exercises. This will help the brain get used to the new reading pattern and learn through it. By playing with these exercises, your brain will speed up and make the progress look seamless.

2. Ancient programming sequence: Many persons expect to read through a document before they can get a grasp of what it says; they expect to see input in grammatical order, that is, from left to right. This is an age long habit and it can have effect on the rate at which we read; this age long sequence is also known as 'talking in your mind'. The brain can understand any meaning without the document being in a grammatical order. Firstly, our thinking is not in any grammatical order.

Let's take this for example, 'me understand you do'. Initially, this sentence takes you off balance because of the grammatical arrangement. But you get to understand it after a second read or a third. Arranged properly, the sentence means 'Do you understand me?

Hence, since reading is basically thinking, then you need to understand that thinking is done in ideas, feelings and images and not necessarily in grammars.

3. Passive reading; Many persons are of the opinion that reading is rather passive and not an active process. However, from outside the reader, reading seems like a passive process. There are many persons who see reading as a passive process. But efficient reading that will increase comprehension needs our mind to be think and do so very fast; we need to think about the subject matter we are reading and relate to the topic properly. It has been proven that avid readers show a lot of brain waves activity in several areas of the brain. Note this

point; if you are not actively criticizing the piece that you read, comparing and feeling same, then all you are doing is a passive reading and it is not effective, this is irrespective of the fact that you are reading fast or not. Activate your mind and do what is right, let your brain get the right response for printed words!

4. Reading words and reading meaning; many expects that only after they have read words, the whole words in a sentence, only then the meaning of what the author is saying will come to mind. They also feel that building words on other words to get enough ideas is how comprehension is attained when reading. Well, this is not the case; this kind of thinking can be linked to the previously mentioned two above. Researchers have shown that the brain can make several connections in non-linear pathways and you are getting comprehension at

a very low rate if your understanding is derived from linear grammatical representation.

This idea can be well demonstrated by the 'chair' analogy. When you look at a chair, you do not first see one leg, then another leg, then another before the seat and the back support. You see at the same time, the whole chair. This is the idea of speed reading, you see the whole. The brain get the idea of the whole chair at a glance! This can happen when you see sentences and paragraphs as a whole.

However, this cannot be achieved rexcept you get a shift in your perception on how to properly comprehend. This particular shift needs, constant practice, repetition, and direction in order to get to comprehend at a higher speed.

There are 2 main challenges when it comes to speed reading.

Firstly, if a persons who wants to learn speed reading is very good in comprehension, he tend to resist and hold themselves back because they may feel the higher speed would affect their comprehension. The solution is just that, learn to free yourself when learning to speed read at high speeds and watch to observe the difference in comprehension.

Secondly, if the learner is very weak and do not get satisfied with their reading rate, they may likely not practice the speed reading skill and quickly pass it off as impossible. One of the popular ways to improve your reading skills is to engage in more reading on diverse subjects than you do not normally read. This allows the brain a better chance of creating more paths pr waves as explained before.

You can surpass the challenge above by getting a better and effective training and a motive to go through the exercise. There may be some uncomfortable experience but that is not the end, try to push on.

Chapter 6
IMPORTANT REASONS WHY YOU SHOULD LEARN SPEED READING

It is a wonderful thing to be able to read very fast and still get the same comprehension level or even higher. Speed reading is something we do need in this 21st century. There are lots of information flooding in daily. And if you want to climb the ladder of success, you have to understand that there is a need to practice speed reading exercises and become efficient in it.

Once you are able to gain the skills of speed reading, you will be able to save a lot of time in doing other things. A lot of information is available for everyone, with thousands of info being churned out daily. And speed reading is a must if you need to meet with the pace of this fast world.

Also, do not give ears to anyone who is of the idea that you can manage your present reading pace as it is and hence there is no need for speed reading. This is a negative motivation, get it out. Stay focused and always put in mind the reason why you want to learn the speed reading habit.

1. It saves time

Speed reading saves lots and lots of time. It helps you create some time else for other things. As a student, you will be able to cover lots of schools works with lesser time and you can catch up with other activities. Also, you do not need to read the whole content before you get the whole idea and comprehend. You can simply skim the page and get the same idea that the person who did the normal slow reading gets.

2. You will get more passion for reading.

When you notice that you can cover more content in a lesser time, reading becomes fun for you and you tend to read often than usual. The driver of a fast vehicle will like to drive his vehicle around than the owner of a slow and faulty cab. The task that you are supposed to complete boringly is now enjoyable and fast. Your ability to think has increased, and you have improved intellectually.

3. It will raise your grades

Since you cover more information faster and also you comprehend faster, you are going to benefit more. Whether as a student or just as a lover of novels; your grades will generally increase and improve, many students have succeeded in improving their grades through the speed reading practice.

See, this whole idea of speed reading is a very interesting act. Once you develop the habit, you are sure going to dig deeper and want to explore various topics. This will help you enrich your knowledge and wealth of creativity. The more you are reading, the better you will increase your speed reading rate. There will be this desire driving you to look for more treasure in books and your desire to know more will be unending.

Anyone who read always get one thing or another, there is no one that losses after reading any book or novel. Knowledge is always gained. Books can be your best friend and you can't be lonely afterwards.

CONCLUSION

Thank you again for buying this book.

I hope this book was able to help you with the necessary steps to improve your reading speed and comprehending faster.

The next step is to create a daily routine to practice all the speed reading exercises as spelt out here. Thanks.

Finally, if you enjoyed this book, then I had like to ask you a favour, would you be kind enough to leave a review for this book? It'd be greatly appreciated.

Thank you!

www.ingramcontent.com/pod-product-compliance
Lightning Source LLC
Chambersburg PA
CBHW070950180426
43194CB00041B/2041